SOURCE MATERIALS FOR ACCOMPANYING, SCORE READING AND TRANSPOSING

Keyboard Strategies

A Piano Series For Group or Private Instruction
Created For the Older Beginner

By Melvin Stecher, Norman Horowitz,
Claire Gordon, R. Fred Kern, and E. L. Lancaster

STECHER &
HOROWITZ
S&H
PIANO LIBRARY

ISBN 978-0-7935-6416-3

G. SCHIRMER, Inc.

DISTRIBUTED BY

HAL•LEONARD®
CORPORATION

7777 W. BLUEMOUND RD. P.O. BOX 13819 MILWAUKEE, WI 53213

PREFACE

The material in SOURCE MATERIALS FOR ACCOMPANYING, SCORE READING AND TRANSPOSING provides students with a variety of music for the study of these functional skills at the keyboard. Pre-college teachers may want to use it with junior high and high school students who serve as vocal, choral and instrumental accompanists.

The following idioms are explored:

1. Chordal Studies and Chorales: This section contains an introduction to four part chorale style reading using music of Bach, Schumann and Gurlitt.
2. Patriotic Songs: This section includes four part settings of America, The Star-Spangled Banner and America, The Beautiful.
3. Vocal and Instrumental Accompaniments: A variety of composers is represented in music for various instruments and voice. There are nine complete pieces or movements from larger works.
4. Score Reading: This section contains choral, orchestral and string quartet scores concentrating mainly on three and four voice open score reading. A special feature is the setting of two Bach fugues from The Well-Tempered Clavier, Book 1 in open score.
5. Orchestral Excerpts for Transposition: Eight familiar orchestral excerpts for a variety of instruments are presented. Students must transpose them to concert pitch. College instrumental majors will be playing many of these examples on their own instruments and will enjoy this application to the keyboard.

SOURCE MATERIALS FOR ACCOMPANYING, SCORE READING AND TRANSPOSING is a reprint of Chapter VII from Master Text II. College teachers may wish to use it in classes to supplement instructional materials from other sources.

CONTENTS

SOURCE MATERIALS FOR ACCOMPANYING, SCORE READING AND TRANSPOSING

I. CHORDAL STUDIES AND CHORALES

PRAYER

Cornelius Gurlitt, Op. 130

6

DAS NEUGEBORNE KINDELEIN

Johann Sebastian Bach

JESU, MEINE FREUDE

Johann Sebastian Bach

CHRIST LAG IN TODESBANDEN

Johann Sebastian Bach

CHORALE - REJOICE, O MY SOUL

Robert Schumann, Op. 68, No. 4

II. PATRIOTIC SONGS

AMERICA

Uncertain origin

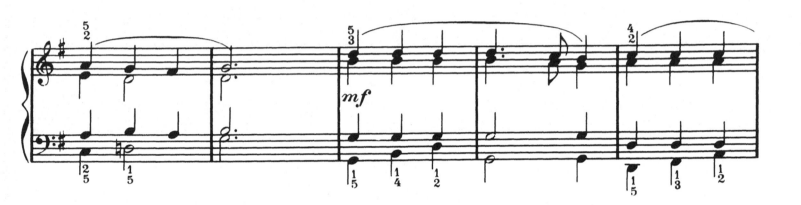

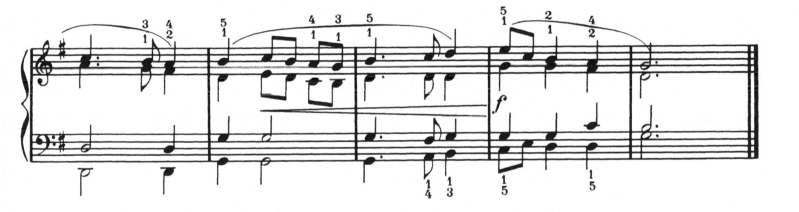

THE STAR-SPANGLED BANNER

John Stafford Smith

AMERICA, THE BEAUTIFUL

Samuel A. Ward

Polonaise

J. S. Bach

Scotch Dance

L. van Beethoven

Fantasie

Gabriel Fauré, Op. 79

from Concerto for Trumpet in E♭ Major

Haydn

from Sonata for Horn and Piano in F Major, Op. 17

Beethoven

Poco adagio, quasi andante

Attacca subito il Rondo

Hedge - Roses.
(HEIDEN - RÖSLEIN.)

FR. SCHUBERT.

Once a boy a wild-rose spied, In the hedge-row grow - ing:
Sah ein Knab' ein Rös-lein steh'n, Rös-lein auf der Hai - den,

Fresh in all her youthful pride, When her beauties he_de-scried, Joy_in his heart was_
war so jung und mor-gen schön, lief er schnell, es nah' zu seh'n, sah's mit_ vie-len_

glow - ing. Lit-tle wild rose, wild-rose red, In the hedge-row grow - ing.
Freu - den. Röslein, Rös-lein, Rös-lein_roth, Röslein auf der Hai - den.

Said the boy "I'll gath-er_thee, In the hedge-row
Kna-be sprach: „ich bre-che dich, Rös-lein auf der

grow - ing!" Said the rose "Then I'll pierce thee That thou may'st re - mem - ber me,
Hai - den!" Rös-lein sprach: „ich ste-che_dich, dass du e - wig denkst an mich,

AUF FLÜGELN DES GESANGES.

"ON WINGS OF SONG."

(Heine.)

Felix Mendelssohn, Op. 34, No. 2.

Andante tranquillo.

war - - - - - - - - - - ten ihr trau - tes Schwester-
pin - - - - - - - - - - ing To greet their sis - ter

rau - - - - - - - - - - schen des heil' - gen Stro-mes
rush - - - - - - - - - - es A - far in sound-ing

lein.
dear.

Well'n.
swells.

1. §. 2.

2. Die   3. Dort
2. The   3. There

wol - len wir nie - der - sin - - ken   un - ter dem Pal - men-
let us lie down and rest us   Un - der a shel - t'ring

Edited by Max Spicker
English version by
Henry G. Chapman

Wiegenlied
(Karl Simrock)
Cradle-Song

Johannes Brahms
Op.49, No.4

Après un Rêve

(From the Tuscan, by Romain Bussine)

After a Dream

English version by
Henry G. Chapman

Gabriel **Fauré**

Tu ray - on - nais comme un ciel é - clai - ré par l'au -
All ra - diant thou as the sky at Au - ro - ra's ap -

ro - - - re; Tu m'ap - pe -
pear - - ing. Thou call - edst

lais et je quit - tais la ter - re Pour m'en - fuir a - vec
me! and to me it was giv - en To de - part from this

toi vers la lu - miè - - - - re;
earth with thee to heav - - - - en;

Les cieux— pour— nous— en - tr'ou-vraient leurs nu - es, Splen -
Then heav'n to— us— did se - crets sur - ren - der, Un -

cresc. poco a poco

deurs_____ in - con - nu - es, Lu - eurs di - vi - nes en - tre -
dream'd_____ of— in splen - dor, Glimps - es of glo - ry, deep— and

cresc. poco a poco

cresc.

vu - es. Hé - las! Hé - las, tris - te ré - veil_ des
ten - der. A - las! a - las! Sad 'tis to wake from

dim.

son - - - - ges, Je t'ap - pel - - le, ô
dream - - - - ing! Ah, re - turn, O

IV. SCORE READING

FUGUE II

Johann Sebastian Bach
from " The Well-Tempered Clavier ", Bk. 1

FUGUE XXI

Johann Sebastian Bach
from "The Well-Tempered Clavier", Bk. 1

from Mass in G

III. Credo

Schubert

15 vi - si - bi - li-um om - ni - um et in - vi - si -

vi - si - bi - li-um om - ni - um et in - vi - si -

vi - si - bi - li-um om - ni - um et in - vi - si -

vi - si - bi - li-um om - ni - um et in - vi - si -

20 bi - li - um.

bi - li - um.

bi - li - um.

bi - li - um.

from Elijah

№ 29. "He, watching over Israel."

Chorus

Mendelssohn

from A German Requium, Op. 45

III

Brahms

Baritone Solo

Lord, make me to know, know the mea-

Andante moderato (♩ = 52)

p

-sure of my days on earth, to con-sid- -er my

frail- ty that I must per- ish, that I must per- ish.

pp

from Messiah

№ 53.- CHORUS

"WORTHY IS THE LAMB THAT WAS SLAIN"

Rev. v: **12,13**

Handel

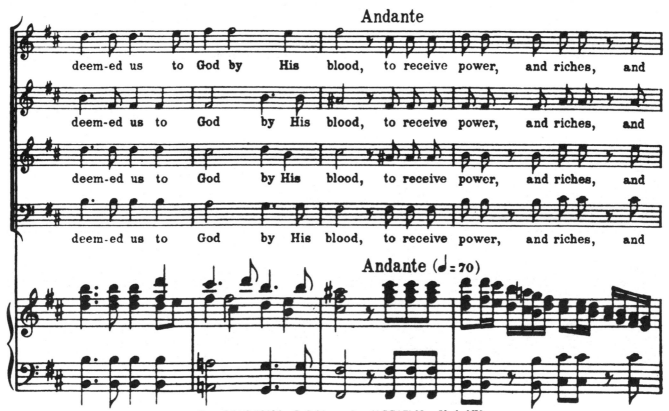

from Symphony No. 7 in A Major, Op. 92

Beethoven

from String Quartet in B Minor, Op. 64, No. 2

Haydn

from String Quartet in D Minor, Op. Posth.

Schubert

II.

Andante con moto.

V. ORCHESTRAL EXCERPTS FOR TRANSPOSITION

1. Symphony No. 3 in E♭ Major, Op. 55 (Eroica)
   3rd Mov't (Trio) - Measures 1 - 18

Horn in E♭ - sounds a major sixth lower than written

Beethoven

2. Pictures at an Exhibition
The Old Castle - Measures 8 - 15
Alto Saxophone in E♭ - sounds a major sixth lower than written

Andante molto cantabile e con dolore

Mussorgsky-Ravel

3. Symphony No. 6 in F Major, Op. 68 (Pastoral)
1st Mov't - Measures 474 - 492
Clarinet in B♭ - sounds a major second lower than written

Beethoven

Allegro ma non troppo

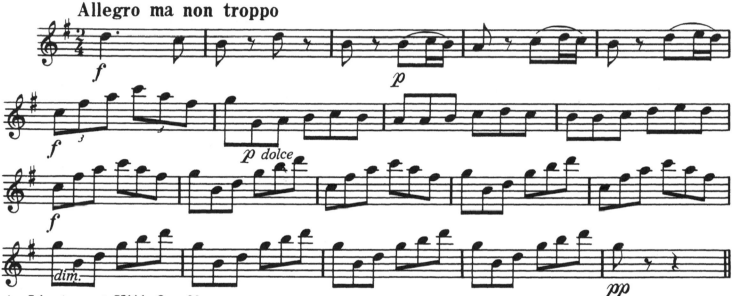

4. Lieutenant Kijé, Op. 60
Troika – Measures 30-52
Tenor Saxophone in B♭ - sounds a major ninth lower than written

Prokofieff

Allegro con brio

5. Symphony No. 5 in E Minor
2nd Mov't - Measures 8 - 28

Horn in F - sounds a perfect fifth lower than written

Tchaikowsky

Andante cantabile, con alcuna licenza

6. Symphony No. 9 in E Minor, Op. 95 (From the New World)
2nd Mov't - Measures 7 - 18

English Horn in F - sounds a perfect fifth lower than written

Dvorak

Largo

7. Symphony No. 4 in E Minor, Op. 98
   2nd Mov't - Measures 4 - 13

Clarinet in A - sounds a minor third lower than written

Brahms

8. Messiah
   The Trumpet Shall Sound - Measures 1 - 28

Trumpet in D - sounds a major second higher than written

Handel